Homegrown:
The Nashville Poems

Homegrown:
The Nashville Poems

Mercedi Surface

Wandering in the Words Press

Copyright © 2018 Mercedi Surface. All rights reserved. No part of this book may be reproduced, stored in a retrieval system, or transmitted in any form or by any means without the prior written consent of the publishers, except by a reviewer who may quote brief passages in a review to be printed in a newspaper, magazine, blog, or journal.

To request permission, visit
www.wanderinginthewordspress.com.

PUBLISHED BY WANDERING IN THE WORDS PRESS

ISBN: 978-0-9991129-4-6

First Edition

To Julie Surface, my sister, oracle, and best friend.
(1982–2015)

ACKNOWLEDGMENTS

I would like to offer my humble gratitude to the following individuals:

Sherrie Montgomery and S. Larama for their kindness and generous contributions to ensuring the success of my dreams, even though we have not yet met.

Stephanie Ryman, Joey Brymer, Diane Corley, Bryan Everett, and Katherine Voss for your generosity to me not only during this project, but for all the times you have taken such good care of me throughout our decades of treasured friendship.

To my fiancé, Rick Prince, whose love and support sustains and elevates me and whose artistic inspiration has breathed new life into the artist within me.

Finally, to my mother, Terry Carlisle, without whose love and support I would not be here today. I love you Mom, and I owe it all to you.

Every book, every poem is medicine.
If it nourishes, assists, or heals one person
it's worth publishing.
—Sandra Cisneros

Introduction | i.
Mercedi y Julie | 2
The Bathtub | 3
Scheherazade | 4
Long Division | 5
Anatomy of the Heart | 6
On Grief | 7
Sisters of the Moon | 8
Conversing with Spirits | 9
Holes | 10
He found God | 11
Close to My Heart | 12
Selecting a Mother | 14
Car Windows at Night | 15
Poetry | 16
Tonight My Grandfather is Smoking a Cigarette with God | 17
My Grandmother's Dresser | 18
Things My Grandmother Used to Say | 19
Judkins | 20
Things on the Lawn | 22

Even Leaves Get the Mulleygrubs | 23

Dusk | 24

Lepidopteraphobia | 25

Caterpillar | 26

Palermo | 27

Soulvision | 28

What's Wrong with this Picture? | 29

Overheard | 30

The Search for Authenticity | 31

My Grandfather's Garden | 32

INTRODUCTION

I am a Nashville native, and will always call Nashville home, even though it feels different to me today than it did growing up. I was born into the microgeneration known as "Xennials," spanning 1977–1983. Being a Xennial means that I had an analog childhood and a digital adulthood. When I was in high school, we had typing class on typewriters, not computers, and at home we stayed connected via newspapers, pagers, and a landline with an answering machine. Embracing technology was a huge leap, as if the world I knew changed overnight.

Nashville has changed tremendously in much the same ways over the last few years. It's always had its own personality as a big city with a small-town feel, and while Southern charm is a hard thing to define, I grew up feeling the richness of it in the friendly faces, hospitality, and give-you-the-shirt-off-his-back types. Nashville's growth has exploded in the past decade, finally "growing into its britches" as my grandmother would say, and finally becoming a big city that *feels* like a big city. Sometimes I feel like not much is the same except the names of the roads.

Growing up a Xennial in the context of having deep Southern roots and through the lens of being lower-middle class blessed me with unique stories to tell. Although I hardly recognize my hometown, I do value the opportunities that are present now for me in making my mark on the world—opportunities that may not have been there before if Nashville had remained "small."

Nashville has been a springboard for many great artists, not only in the music industry but also international multimedia creators such as Oprah who, incidentally, went to East High School with my mother. Oprah has become one of my heroes for her having overcome hardship in her formative years and having gone on to really make her mark on the world. She did so with the utmost love and grace, as well as an inner light that seems to serve as a compass and get brighter with each passing year. I want that for my life. Oprah was not content to remain small, and I think Nashville's growth has caused me to realize that neither am I.

This book is a collection of my reflections on growing up in the South, as well as observations on family, grief, and the poetry we call life. It is my deepest wish that the words I have put to paper as a result of these experiences will bring those who read them comfort and connection but most of all that sense of joy that one gets from experiencing another's art—because art, whether it is written, visual, or musical is truly one of those beautiful things that makes this life worth living.

Mercedi y Julie

I.
Julie, wake up! Mom just told me there is no Santa.
(I shake her awake, with tears, in the dark.)

Shut up, Stupid. I know. And you are supposed to be the "big" sister.

Julie, the world as I know it is lost and I am only 8.
She rolls over so that I cannot see her tears and pretends not to care.

II.
Days go by and I do not hear from her. She is living up north,
the first of us to move from our hometown.
She goes door-to-door selling coupon books.

I wait tables, and a man asks what do you really do? I tell him this is it.
He responds, "So you are just a regular old waitress?" and I quit.

III.
An antique Santa, with cotton beard frayed by time,
vacuumed up into the sky with the attic,
along with all of the memories one keeps there.
It was not the last of precious things never thought to be lost so soon.

Julie, life seems unfair.
(I write to her in a journal in which I keep her memory alive.)

"I know." She replies from somewhere far, far away.
I roll over and pretend not to care, hoping she cannot see my tears.

The Bathtub

I pace the house with distracted thoughts
then I sit in the bathtub and stare emptily
at the knobs labeled *Hot, Hot, and Cold,*
suddenly angry at the plumber or contractor
responsible
for this irresponsibility
for this laziness
for this blatant disregard for
The Way Things Should Be.

The world hasn't made much sense to me over the past week—
the brunt
of my grief
weighted
and simultaneously
suspended
by big words such as
autopsy and
toxicology report
and by the time it takes for these to come to pass.
The familiar workings of my day
all seem to move now in an unrecognizable fashion.

As questions swirl into a downward spiral
I collect my energies and try to force my hurt
to follow them down the drain.

Scheherazade

Life is not a support-system for art. It's the other way around.
—Stephen King

I used to think that life was hard,
that every year was a thief,
out to steal various prized possessions . . .
slowly plundering my joy,
until a master thief-year finally absconded with my essence.
Now I see beauty in the most awful of things:
from a drawer in the morgue
my sister's face—a Monet painting.
The dappled purples, reds, and blues
tell the stories of her life.
Stories of separation, abuse, addiction,
but also of love, of boundless generosity and wit in spite of it all
and most importantly, the end of long suffering.
By virtue of our craft, the ordinary, boring, or unpleasant
has a chance to become beautiful.
Through the aperture of an open heart we adjust our perception,
carefully reframing darkness into light,
transmuting pain into joy so that we may keep going.
Now I tell my stories
to save my own life.

Long Division

Sitting in our favorite Indian restaurant,
I have Sag Paneer alone
and stare at all the people
who are not you.

I think of how you were so good at math,
and how we were going to combine our talents,
merging numbers and words
to become an expert sister-astrologer-team,
operating as we did best
as two halves of the same whole.

Everyday activities are now colored by loss;
future activities already wear a patina of sadness.
I still read your horoscope every morning.
You are transforming it says, going on a journey.

It is evident that your passing
has not diminished your arithmetic skills
because what is death
but another form of long division?

Anatomy of the Heart

When watching a loved one make hard decisions such as
whether to eat or to breathe
it becomes clear to my prefrontal cortex that
there won't be many decisions left to make
after this.

I couldn't really hear anything past "heart failure"
besides my blood rushing to relocate . . .
my own valves and ventricles
suddenly making their way north of the clavicle—
edging out my larynx,
which I didn't need at that moment anyway.

It's a peculiar thing how the observer inside of us
will hang onto one insignificant nugget of nothingness
in times of traumatic stress:
the rarely noticed landscape of the back of one's own hand,
the ugly design of the waiting room carpet,
or a strange call to arms over the doctor's statement
about the heart as the body's most important organ.
It occurs to me that he is right, of course.
However, if mine had been working properly,
I would have supposed it was the brain.

On Grief

After the doctor makes you aware of death's presence, the ride home is eerie.
Although unseen, I can feel him next to me in the ether
like a hitchhiker I didn't stop for
but somehow got in anyway
and now we ride along in a fearful, uncomfortable silence.

The radio plays the saddest possible songs
as a soundtrack to my melancholy.
The dark passenger is choosing the selection
and I'm too afraid to tell him not to touch the dial
or to change the station.

Branches on bushes along the sides of the road reach out to me, then bow
it is clear that they knew all along.
Their silent gesture
says, "We're sorry,"
"We're sorry."

Sisters of the Moon

The moon is a shiny coin
given for good behavior.
Every night it is tossed, like a wish,
into the deep black well of the sky.

You left early one Friday morning in September.
I did not get to say goodbye
before you tossed yourself up into that deep black well.
I don't think even you knew you were leaving.

I like the moon
because it illuminates things unseen in the daylight
and because when I call out to you from a sleep thick with dreams
it is in her silvery voice that you answer.

Conversing with Spirits

Today I don't feel like writing
but I ask that the creative spirits
come and knock on my door anyway.
I invite them in to share a cup of tea.
"I just lost my sister," I say.
Unaccustomed, I assume, to the parlance of this world
they reply,
"Well, go find her."

I tell them they do not understand
but they assure me that they do
and then declare,
"You will find her.
We will help."

Holes

My father was stabbed over a pool game at 3 Crow Bar
and left to bleed out on the curb
only then it was called The Long Branch Saloon.
There were bullet holes in the ceiling.

That same night, a cab driver saw a bloody mess
on the corner of Woodland and 11th and did the right thing.
He stopped and dragged into his cab a misfortunate man
whose stomach was full of holes.

Twenty-five years later,
a man came into the golf course where my mother worked.
He asked about her last name and went on to say
that the name was so unusual he never could forget it.

He then recounted a night when he used to drive a cab
and dropped off a dying man at the emergency room.
"I saved that man's life," he said.
"But he ruined my cab."

He Found God

After school I read the letter.
For the last six months of my childhood
I would be eligible for the Social Security Benefits
of one James Surface.
My sister and I sat silent and motionless,
watching streetlights pass like damp orbs against the black February cold
from the backseat of my grandparent's station wagon.
My mother, remarried, refused to attend.
In the dimly lit room I was introduced to
distant aunts, cousins, and half-siblings
including a dirty-looking "sister" with no teeth.
I have a sister who has no teeth?
In the casket, he looked different
than in all the pictures.
I was told he had turned his life around, just before.
It was the first time I had ever seen him.

Close to My Heart

Forever visiting the cardiologist,
my best friend and constant companion:
a stuffed bear that came with the cloth diapers
recommended for the heart patients.
Dy-dee Bear.
The formerly shiny glass of his eyes
scratched to a milky opaque.
His denim nose, frayed, like the jeans I have on now,
his fur matted to the texture of a favorite fleece sweatshirt.
The red heart on his chest had a crack
to match the hole in mine and
he wore a cloth diaper too.
He listened to every sound I uttered
until one blustery day his ear came loose
and blew down Eastland Avenue.

Some part of me presently
must have been able to speak backwards through time,
and looking into the face of my grandmother,
implore her . . .
for all the EKGs,
heart-stress tests
and staples in my chest,
I had enough that was broken.
Please don't let it be . . .

I have never seen an old woman run so fast.
Today Dy-Dee Bear looks at me
through cataract'd eyes
with two ears,
keeping me company when I feel the need
to sit in the basement and talk to old things.

Selecting a Mother

Soft as the voice of an angel, breathing a lesson unheard
Hope with a gentle persuasion, whispers her comforting word
Wait till the darkness is over, wait till the tempest is done
Hope for the sunshine tomorrow, after the shower is gone

Whispering hope oh how welcome Thy voice
Making my heart in its sorrow rejoice

—*Septimus Winner, 1868*

I must have come into this world
searching for a mother who would incite my penchant
for the melancholy side of life
and simultaneously cause me to love words—
their intricacies, clarity, and equivocality,
more than man has ever loved a thing.
As my mother rocked me, the words to the hymns she sang conjured
strange and haunting images:
a huge angel, looming over my shoulder, intimidating me;
a small and dainty woman named Hope, who endeavors to protect me;
the fear of the nighttime, waiting for my father to get out of the shower
so that all of this terror would end.
And finally, as a presumed reward for my troubles,
on a hill somewhere far, far away
I would trade an old rugged cross for a crown.

Car Windows at Night

Raindrop streetlight firework alchemy—
tiny amber explosions roll into one another
against the rat-a-tat-tat.
My sister and I write our names and draw flowers
then play tic-tac-toe in the condensation.
Using the sleeves of our coats, we wipe it all away and
then force heat from our mouths close to the glass,
impatient for the canvas to return.
Mother lights a cigarette;
we watch it glow in the darkness.
Crack the window, Mommy.
It is not beautiful like the tumbling fireworks.
Bored, we press our foreheads to the pane,
waiting to be lulled to sleep by the engine's steady vibrato
as the cricket legs on the windshield chirp away the rain.

Poetry

Poetry looks like two children with the same heart defect
born to two people with the same substance abuse problem,
like a grandparent's love when Mother is in rehab with Johnny Cash
and Father is nowhere.

Poetry looks like the kind face of the man from church
bringing baskets of fresh cheese and fruit and a stocking with toys
to a single mom of two at Christmas.

Poetry looks like the neighborhood I grew up in…
a cop on the left of us who thinks we don't know that his "girlfriend," Sugar,
is a hooker.
To the right, a devout Mormon lady
whose fiancé likes to stand over my mom and talk while she sunbathes.
The two obese women from Kentucky who say they are mother and daughter
but may be sisters or lesbians or both.
And the little girl across the street who, at nine years old, is smoking cigarettes
and holding up her dress to show her panties to the passing cars.

Tonight My Grandfather is Smoking a Cigarette with God

Tonight my grandfather is smoking a cigarette with God
in his blue work suit, with its row of pens
in the left breast pocket.
In a moment he will settle into the big easy chair
and he and God will watch the evening news.

As my grandmother made dinner
I sat on the kitchen floor threading buttons on a string
while my mother, away, purged demons at the clinic.

A grandparent's love is beautiful, necessary,
and sometimes too much weight on too little thread,
to put a smile on the face of a child who does not know she is poor
because what are buttons
but instruments of holding together?

Somewhere out in the ether
my grandmother is making minute-steak and cornbread
for God,
for my grandfather
and perhaps, for me.

My Grandmother's Dresser

A bottle of Estée
atop a mirrored tray
her signature scent and
possibly her favorite thing
or maybe ours

A dusty box of Kleenex
and even a rolled pair of socks
it has been how long since the funeral?
and yet we cannot bring ourselves
to move treasures such as these

I read once that Ms. Lauder had noticed the light
from two crystal chandeliers
shimmering in her champagne glass
and thought how wonderful it would be
to capture that image in a fragrance

It's no wonder that my grandmother
was attracted to the scent
for I think that God must have noticed that too
and thought how wonderful it would be
to capture that in a person

Things My Grandmother Used to Say

Some rules on living as per my grandmother:
On self-esteem:
I'm a lady and expect to be treated like one.
On privacy:
It's my house, I'll do as I damn well please.
When life lets you down:
Hold your head up high and go on
and even when
your get up and go's done got up and went
you must
walk in like you own the place.
On the paranormal:
It's not the ghosts and dead you need to fear but the living.
On properly setting one straight:
He'll know he's been talked to when I get through with him.
There is some inescapable wisdom that I have found in her simple maxims.
Hard work's good for you.
On that note, if you will please excuse me,
I must go clean the bathroom now because
You can always tell how clean a person is by looking at the base of their commode.

Judkins

Mrs. Judkins lived with her husband in the quadplex
one house over from my grandparents.
She gave my sister and me coins
and sometimes food
when we'd visit.
Her unit was hot and smelled like old people.
I always felt awkward
when my grandmother made me go over there alone.

Judkins liked to sew
and in the summertime
she had yard sales for the sole purpose
of selling her handmade throw pillows.
She must have done well with this
because she had them every weekend.

Judkins didn't drive, only rode the city bus.
Once we took the bus with her downtown
to shop at Woolco.

At some point Mr. Judkins died,
and she lived as a widow.
Mr. Judkins' room became the sewing room
and was filled to the ceiling with throw pillows.
She sewed our Easter dresses one year—
the most embarrassing explosion
of satin and taffeta and lace—
and the year the collectible Happy Holidays Barbie came out
we got the Judkins version because we couldn't afford the real thing.

We didn't visit Judkins much as we got older.
She went a little crazy near the end,
in her eighties and claiming
that the 35-year-old bus driver was her boyfriend.
The yard sales stopped
and the trips to Woolco became more frequent.

My family liked to sit around my grandmother's kitchen table
smoking cigarettes while talking about the neighbors.
One day I overheard my grandmother mention
that Judkins died and that there had been no one
to attend any funeral.

At that moment, a small piece of my heart set sail
in a little satin boat with a coin in it.
Who made the burial arrangements?
And what did they do with all those throw pillows?

Things on the Lawn

I just got off the phone with my mother.
We talked about the tornado that came through in '98,
which took down the house we both grew up in
and most of the trees in East Nashville.
Fragments of our lives littered the lawn—
my aunt's megaphone from her days of cheerleading at East High,
an antique clock with a tiny ballerina inside
(who stopped spinning circa 1960),
glitter and tinsel, a widowed Mrs. Claus and an orphaned baby Jesus
and other holiday decorations that dwelled in what used to be the attic.
Vice President Gore was on the lawn too,
with his Secret Service team in crisp white shirts and black pants,
there to assess the damage.
One man approached my uncle, also in a crisp white shirt and black pants,
and asked if he had seen a fellow agent.
The words in his reply were surely irrelevant—
his thick East Tennessee drawl was certainly the tip-off
that he was not one of them.

Even Leaves Get the Mulleygrubs

I read once that,
to fix a case of the mulleygrubs,
one should put on a red dress.
So here I sit in my red dress
on my front porch stoop, with my head in my hands
lazing like a cat in the warm November sun.
A funny sight I must be to the passers-by
in a beautiful red dress on a dilapidated porch step.

The cracks in the paint
resemble Earth from a distance,
if only the Earth were a faded gray-blue.
And the smaller cracks:
a forgotten language
in the mouths of people as small as I am to God.

There is an overturned leaf off the coast of Denmark
and a bird's white turd in the Indian Ocean—
surely alarming in size to any passing ships.

A frantic ant makes his way swiftly
beyond the Arabian and Malay Peninsulas.

A gentle hurricane lifts a corner of the leaf,
and I can see that on the front
it is the same color as my dress.

Dusk

There is something very sultry about the dusk.
A beautiful lady, readying herself to make love to the night:
a light dusting of powder,
an elegant spritz of seductive perfume,
a slender thigh exposed as fingers adjust a stocking . . .
she meets her lover: dark, handsome, lustful, robust.
She loses herself in him.
A torrid affair so intoxicating, so compelling,
they indulge every evening
never questioning why morning finds both alone.

Lepidopteraphobia

You have them all duped—
your spell shall not be cast on me.
Look at you, you ugly winged harpy.
A harbinger of life's last call,
you swoop in and stun with your supposed beauty.
Eeriest of abductors, my soul you shall never have.
Look at the way you molest those flowers!
And to think that society condones you.
Balanced on your accosting perch, the terrifying extent
of your patterned sorcery is revealed on your back.
Like the Reaper's own breath, I can see the dust of decay
blown forth from your wings as they creak open
and then snap suddenly shut
as if on an antique door not meant to be opened
or the final closure of life's most precious book.
Never believe for one moment that I cannot see this.

Caterpillar

Oh fuzziest of things
Cute as a baby with your black shiny head
Until you do that mummification thing
And out comes the wing-ed demon.

Palermo

There is an old mallard who laughs at me in the morning.
I call him Palermo.
BAH HA HA HAAAAAA,
he says.
Unlike the other ducks who quack and wonk and rurp,
Palermo's call is resonating, long and gravelly,
with an almost clicking quality
like the turn of a torque wrench.
As I round the pond on my morning stroll I hear him,
heckling me from the audience.
In a past life I see him: an ornery old man in a fedora,
halfheartedly laughing from the side of his mouth
as he leans over his scotch,
squinting his eyes and taking a pull from his cigar.
Palermo's laugh rolls into a cough—
that's what a duck will get for smoking a pack a day for over 20 years.
I really don't mind that Palermo laughs at me.
In fact, I like it because it makes me laugh too.

Soulvision

From a young age I have experienced a feeling—
like a déjà vu of a déjà vu,
a vision of half-sleep,
hypnogogic dreamlets impressed upon
the threshold of my consciousness.

When I was younger
and had nothing to do but watch
the patterns on the backs of my eyelids,
I was entranced by the form constant.
I thought I was looking at cells.

Visions of tiny yellow dots with black centers,
sometimes morphing into spaces between orbs,
flashing and undulating like some neurogenic peristalsis.

A nameless, timeless essence in pursuit of me
cushioning me in a hushed orchid light.
As pupils overtake the iris, my eyes can't focus.
The only sound like the inside of a heartbeat alarm clock,
muffled and repetitive from inside this cavernous womb.

Like a bulging drop of water—
consciousness on the head of a pin—
my spirit braces for the plunge
as gravity compels this new awareness to burst forth.

What's Wrong with this Picture?

Recently I have seen an unusual number of morbidly obese men
smooshed behind the wheel of a Smart Car
with a cigarette hanging out of their mouths.

This says to me any combination of the following:
Those who wish to take care of the environment
do not wish to take care of their bodies.

The eco-conscious folk
love food just as much as they love the environment.

Or possibly that the Smart Car is so tiny
that it makes any normal person
look like a marshmallow shoved into a thimble.

Overheard

I am taking a walk outside.
A man is putting away his tools in the back of a big red pickup truck.
He is talking on his phone
and must be discussing some pro-bono construction work
or attempting to discourage his friend from taking the job
because he says
Yehbutheeaintgunuhpayyuhnuthindadooeet
in one long sing-song breath as I walk past.

The Search for Authenticity

I have made it my mission to scour the varnish off of this life.
To scrub and scrub until I am stuck by the splinters.

To boil it down and see what is left
in the resulting resin.

To turn every last knob, open every last door
and peel back the last of the coverings.

To poke it, prod it, subject it to the most potent truth serum
and smear it on a slide.

To dry it out in the sun
and eat the seeds.

My Grandfather's Garden

My grandfather was a gunner's mate in WWII
but never talked about it.
What he did talk about were the important things in life:
how to grow the perfect tomato,
how to recognize a brown recluse,
and repeatedly informing me that if I didn't stop biting my nails
I'd never get a boyfriend.
To this day, no tomato can match my Paw-Paw's tomato.

Somewhere between
the constant examining of spiders' backs beneath a magnifying glass
and trying to keep my fingers out of my mouth
I absorbed the secret to gardening.
The soil may not be quality, and the conditions may not be perfect
and it may not even look like much on the outside,
but it's still going to produce the sweetest fruit you've ever tasted
because it's grown with love.

Nashville is not the same as it used to be.
The roots I sprouted from were quite different roots
and the conditions were certainly not perfect.
My life may not look like much on the outside,
but it's the sweetest life I've ever tasted and
I'm proud to say I'm homegrown.

Life loves the person who dares to live it.
—Maya Angelou

www.ingramcontent.com/pod-product-compliance
Lightning Source LLC
Chambersburg PA
CBHW050449010526
44118CB00013B/1754